Mars Climate Orbiter
Phase I Report

Mishap Investigation Board

Enhanced with Text Analytics by

PageKicker Robot Fast Hans

Summary

Most statistically significant sentences as identified by PageKicker.

- The MCO MIB has determined that the root cause for the loss of the MCO spacecraft was the failure to use metric units in the coding of a ground software file, "Small Forces," used in trajectory models.
- Verification and validation process did not adequately address ground software MPL Recommendations: • Verify the consistent use of units throughout the MPL spacecraft design and operations • Conduct software audit for specification compliance on all data transferred between JPL and Lockheed Martin Astronautics • Verify Small Forces models used for MPL • Compare prime MPL navigation projections with projections by alternate navigation methods • Train Navigation Team in spacecraft design and operations • Prepare for possibility of executing trajectory correction maneuver number 5 • Establish MPL systems organization to concentrate on trajectory correction maneuver number 5 and entry, descent and landing operations • Take steps to improve communications 7
- MPL Recommendations (Continued): • Augment Operations Team staff with experienced people to support entry, descent and landing • Train entire MPL Team and encourage use of Incident, Surprise, Anomaly process • Develop and execute systems verification matrix for all requirements • Conduct independent reviews on all mission critical events • Construct a fault tree analysis for remainder of MPL mission • Assign overall Mission Manager • Perform thermal analysis of thrusters feedline heaters and consider use of pre-conditioning pulses • Reexamine propulsion subsystem operations during entry, descent, and landing
- The missions were the Mars Climate Orbiter (MCO) and the Mars Polar Lander (MPL).
- MCO Root Cause The MCO MIB has determined that the root cause for the loss of the MCO spacecraft was the failure to use metric units in the coding of a ground software file, "Small Forces," used in trajectory models.
- Critical information on the control and desaturation of the MCO momentum was not passed on to the operations navigation team.
- There were a number of opportunities for the systems engineering organization to identify the units problem leading to mission loss of MCO.. The lack of an adequate systems engineering function contributed to the lack of understanding on the part of the navigation team of essential spacecraft design characteristics and the spacecraft team understanding of the navigation challenge.
- 5: Communications Among Project Elements In the MCO project, and again in the MPL project, there is evidence of inadequate communications between the project elements, including the development and operations teams, the operations navigation and operations teams, the project management and technical teams, and the project and technical line management.
- In addition, the spacecraft operations team did not understand the concerns of the operations navigation team.
- MPL Recommendation: The Board recommends that the MPL operations navigation team receive proper training in the spacecraft design and operations.

- MPL Recommendation: The Board recommends that the MPL project clarify roles and responsibilities for all individuals on the team.

Readability Report

```
Flesh-Kincaid Grade Level:    13.31
Flesh Reading Ease Score:     34.20
Sentences:                    586
Words:                        11,359
Averaage Syllables per Word:  1.81
Average Words per Sentence:   19.38
```

Dramatis Personae:
Arthur G. Stephenson
Dr. Daniel R. Mulville
Dr. Peter Norvig
Dr. Edward J. Weiler

Gazetteer:
Mars Climate Orbiter
Mars Polar Lander
MPL Terminal Descent Maneuver
MCO
George C. Marshall Space Flight Center

Miscellany:
MCO Board
MCO
Operations Navigation Team
Mission Operations
Mars Surveyor Operations Project
Mars Global Surveyor
development team
Jet Propulsion Laboratory
National Aeronautics and Space Administration
Mars Surveyor Project
MCO Program Executive
Angular Momentum Desaturation
EDL
MPL
JPL
MCO Flight Operations Manager
Mars Orbit Insertion
MOI
MPL Team
NPG
JPL MCO
Lander Science
software development
Lockheed Martin Astronautics
NASA MCO
Navigation Specialist
Independent Reviews
Mars Surveyor Operations
Mission Operations Directorate
AMD
Flight Operations Manager
Navigation Team
SIS
Associate Administrator
Flight Design
ΔV
ISA
Johns Hopkins University

Figure A. Wordcloud.

Mars Climate Orbiter

Mishap Investigation Board

Phase I Report

November 10, 1999

Table of Contents

Mars Climate Orbiter Mishap Investigation Board
Phase I Report

Signature Page

_____/s/_____
Arthur G. Stephenson
Chairman
George C. Marshall Space Flight Center
Director

_____/s/_____
Dr. Daniel R. Mulville
Chief Engineer
NASA Headquarters

_____/s/_____
Frank H. Bauer
Chief, Guidance, Navigation and Control
Center
Goddard Space Flight Center

_____/s/_____
Greg A. Dukeman
Guidance and Navigation Specialist
Vehicle Flight Mechanics Group
George C. Marshall Space Flight Center

_____/s/_____
Dr. Peter Norvig
Chief, Computational Sciences Division
Ames Research Center

_____/s/_____
Approved
Dr. Edward J. Weiler
Associate Administrator
Office of Space Science

_____/s/_____
Lia S. LaPiana
Executive Secretary
Program Executive
Office of Space Science
NASA Headquarters

_____/s/_____
Dr. Peter J. Rutledge (ex-officio)
Director, Enterprise Safety and
Mission Assurance Division
NASA Headquarters

_____/s/_____
David Folta
System Engineer, Guidance,
Navigation and Control Center
Goddard Space Flight Center

_____/s/_____
Robert Sackheim
Assistant Director for Space
Propulsion Systems
George C. Marshall Space Flight Center

_____/s/_____
Approved
Frederick D. Gregory
Associate Administrator
Office of Safety and Mission Assurance

Advisors:
Office of Chief Counsel: MSFC/Louis Durnya
Office of Public Affairs: HQs/Douglas M. Isbell

Consultants

Ann Merwarth	NASA/GSFC-retired Expert in ground operations & flight software development
Moshe F. Rubinstein	Prof. Emeritus, University of California, Los Angeles Civil and environmental engineering
John Mari	Vice-President of Product Assurance Lockheed Martin Astronautics
Peter Sharer	Senior Professional Staff Mission Concepts and Analysis Group The Johns Hopkins University Applied Physics Laboratory
Craig Staresinich	Chandra X-ray Observatory Program Manager TRW
Dr. Michael G. Hauser	Deputy Director Space Telescope Science Institute
Tim Crumbley	Deputy Group Lead Flight Software Group Avionics Department George C. Marshall Space Flight Center
Don Pearson	Assistant for Advanced Mission Design Flight Design and Dynamics Division Mission Operations Directorate Johnson Space Center

Acknowledgements

The Mars Climate Orbiter Mishap Investigation Board wishes to thank the technical teams from Jet Propulsion Laboratory (JPL) and Lockheed Martin Astronautics for their cooperation which was essential in our review of the Mars Climate Orbiter and Mars Polar Lander projects. Special thanks to Lia LaPiana and Frank Bauer for pulling this report together with the support of the entire Board and consultants.

Executive Summary

This Phase I report addresses paragraph 4.A. of the letter establishing the Mars Climate Orbiter (MCO) Mishap Investigation Board (MIB) (Appendix). Specifically, paragraph 4.A. of the letter requests that the MIB focus on any aspects of the MCO mishap which must be addressed in order to contribute to the Mars Polar Lander's safe landing on Mars. The Mars Polar Lander (MPL) entry-descent-landing sequence is scheduled for December 3, 1999.

This report provides a top-level description of the MCO and MPL projects (section 1), it defines the MCO mishap (section 2) and the method of investigation (section 3) and then provides the Board's determination of the MCO mishap root cause (section 4), the MCO contributing causes (section 5) and MCO observations (section 6). Based on the MCO root cause, contributing causes and observations, the Board has formulated a series of recommendations to improve the MPL operations. These are included in the respective sections. Also, as a result of the Board's review of the MPL, specific observations and associated recommendations pertaining to MPL are described in section 7. The plan for the Phase II report is described in section 8. The Phase II report will focus on the processes used by the MCO mission, develop lessons learned, and make recommendations for future missions.

The MCO Mission objective was to orbit Mars as the first interplanetary weather satellite and provide a communications relay for the MPL which is due to reach Mars in December 1999. The MCO was launched on December 11, 1998, and was lost sometime following the spacecraft's entry into Mars occultation during the Mars Orbit Insertion (MOI) maneuver. The spacecraft's carrier signal was last seen at approximately 09:04:52 UTC on Thursday, September 23, 1999.

The MCO MIB has determined that the root cause for the loss of the MCO spacecraft was the failure to use metric units in the coding of a ground software file, "Small Forces," used in trajectory models. Specifically, thruster performance data in English units instead of metric units was used in the software application code titled SM_FORCES (small forces). A file called Angular Momentum Desaturation (AMD) contained the output data from the SM_FORCES software. The data in the AMD file was required to be in metric units per existing software interface documentation, and the trajectory modelers assumed the data was provided in metric units per the requirements.

During the 9-month journey from Earth to Mars, propulsion maneuvers were periodically performed to remove angular momentum buildup in the on-board reaction wheels (flywheels). These Angular Momentum Desaturation (AMD) events occurred 10-14 times more often than was expected by the operations navigation team. This was because the MCO solar array was asymmetrical relative to the spacecraft body as compared to Mars Global Surveyor (MGS) which had symmetrical solar arrays. This asymmetric effect significantly increased the Sun-induced (solar pressure-induced) momentum buildup on the spacecraft. The increased AMD events coupled with the fact that the angular momentum (impulse) data was in English, rather than metric, units, resulted in small errors being introduced in the trajectory estimate over the course of the 9-month journey. At the time of Mars insertion, the spacecraft trajectory was approximately 170 kilometers lower than planned. As a result, MCO either was destroyed in the atmosphere or re-entered heliocentric space after leaving Mars' atmosphere.

The Board recognizes that mistakes occur on spacecraft projects. However, sufficient processes are usually in place on projects to catch these mistakes before they become critical to mission success. Unfortunately for MCO, the root cause was not caught by the processes in-place in the MCO project.

A summary of the findings, contributing causes and MPL recommendations are listed below. These are described in more detail in the body of this report along with the MCO and MPL observations and recommendations.

Root Cause: Failure to use metric units in the coding of a ground software file, "Small Forces," used in trajectory models

Contributing Causes: 1. Undetected mismodeling of spacecraft velocity changes
2. Navigation Team unfamiliar with spacecraft
3. Trajectory correction maneuver number 5 not performed
4. System engineering process did not adequately address transition from development to operations
5. Inadequate communications between project elements
6. Inadequate operations Navigation Team staffing
7. Inadequate training
8. Verification and validation process did not adequately address ground software

MPL Recommendations:
- Verify the consistent use of units throughout the MPL spacecraft design and operations
- Conduct software audit for specification compliance on all data transferred between JPL and Lockheed Martin Astronautics
- Verify Small Forces models used for MPL
- Compare prime MPL navigation projections with projections by alternate navigation methods
- Train Navigation Team in spacecraft design and operations
- Prepare for possibility of executing trajectory correction maneuver number 5
- Establish MPL systems organization to concentrate on trajectory correction maneuver number 5 and entry, descent and landing operations
- Take steps to improve communications

MPL Recommendations (Continued):
- Augment Operations Team staff with experienced people to support entry, descent and landing
- Train entire MPL Team and encourage use of Incident, Surprise, Anomaly process
- Develop and execute systems verification matrix for all requirements
- Conduct independent reviews on all mission critical events
- Construct a fault tree analysis for remainder of MPL mission
- Assign overall Mission Manager
- Perform thermal analysis of thrusters feedline heaters and consider use of pre-conditioning pulses
- Reexamine propulsion subsystem operations during entry, descent, and landing

1. Mars Climate Orbiter (MCO) and Mars Polar Lander (MPL) Project Descriptions

In 1993, NASA started the Mars Surveyor program with the objective of con ducting an on-going series of missions to explore Mars. The Jet Propulsion Laboratory (JPL) was identified as the lead center for this program. Mars Global Surveyor (MGS) was identified as the first flight mission, with a launch date in late 1996. In 1995, two additional missions were identified for launch in late 1998/early 1999. The missions were the Mars Climate Orbiter (MCO) and the Mars Polar Lander (MPL). JPL created the Mars Surveyor Project '98 (MSP '98) office with the responsibility to define the missions, develop both spacecraft and all payload elements, and integrate/test/launch both flight systems. In addition, the Program specified that the Mars Surveyor Operations Project (MSOP) would be responsible for conducting flight operations for both MCO and MPL as well as the MGS.

The MSP '98 Development Project used a prime contract vehicle to support project implementation. Lockheed Martin Astronautics (LMA) of Denver, Colorado was selected as the prime contractor. LMA's contracted development responsibilities were to design and develop both spacecraft, lead flight system integration and test, and support launch operations. JPL retained responsibilities for overall project management, spacecraft and instrument development management, project system engineering, mission design, navigation design, mission operation system development, ground data system development, and mission assurance. The MSP '98 project assigned the responsibility for mission operations systems/ground data systems (MOS/GDS) development to the MSOP, LMA provided support to MSOP for MOS/GDS development tasks related to spacecraft test and operations.

The MCO was launched December 11, 1998, and the MPL was launched January 3, 1999. Both were launched atop identical Delta II launch vehicles from Launch Complex 17 A and B at Cape Canaveral Air Station, Florida, carrying instruments to map the planet's surface, profile the structure of the atmosphere, detect surface ice reservoirs and dig for traces of water beneath Mars' rusty surface.

The lander also carries a pair of basketball-sized microprobes. These microprobes will be released as the lander approaches Mars and will dive toward the planet's surface, penetrating up to about 1 meter underground to test 10 new technologies, including a science instrument to search for traces of water ice. The microprobe project, called Deep Space 2, is part of NASA's New Millennium Program.

These missions were the second installment in NASA's long-term program of robotic exploration of Mars, which was initiated with the 1996 launches of the currently orbiting Mars Global Surveyor and the Mars Pathfinder lander and rover.

The MSOP assumed responsibility for both MCO and MPL at launch. MSOP is implemented in a partnering mode in which distinct operations functions are performed by a geographically distributed set of partners. LMA performs all spacecraft operations functions including health and status monitoring and spacecraft sequence development. In addition, LMA performs real time command and monitoring operations from their facility in Denver, Colorado. JPL is responsible for overall project and mission management, system engineering, quality assurance, GDS maintenance, navigation, mission planning, and sequence integration. Each of the science teams is responsible for planning and sequencing their instrument observations, processing and archiving the resulting data, and performing off line data analysis. These operations are typically performed at the Principal Investigator's home institution. MSOP personnel are also currently supporting MGS operations.

Nine and a half months after launch, in September 1999, MCO was to fire its main engine to achieve an elliptical orbit around Mars. See figure 1. The spacecraft was to then skim through Mars' upper atmosphere for several weeks in a technique called aerobraking to reduce velocity and move into a circular orbit. Friction against the spacecraft's single, 5.5-meter solar array was to have slowed the spacecraft as it dipped into the atmosphere each orbit, reducing its orbit period from more than 14 hours to 2 hours. On September 23, 1999 the MCO mission was lost when it entered the Martian atmosphere on a lower than expected trajectory.

MPL is scheduled to land on Mars on December 3, 1999, 2 to 3 weeks after the orbiter was to have finished aerobraking. The lander is aimed toward a target sector within the edge of the layered terrain near Mars' south pole.

Like Mars Pathfinder, MPL will dive directly into the Martian atmosphere, using an aeroshell and parachute scaled down from Pathfinder's design to slow its initial descent. See figures 2 and 3. The smaller MPL will not use airbags, but instead will rely on onboard guidance, radar, and retro-rockets to land softly on the layered terrain near the south polar cap a few weeks after the seasonal carbon dioxide frosts have disappeared. After the heat shield is jettisoned, a camera will take a series of pictures of the landing site as the spacecraft descends.

As it approaches Mars, about 10 minutes before touchdown, the lander will release the two Deep Space 2 microprobes. Once released, the projectiles will collect atmospheric data before they crash at about 200 meters per second and bury themselves beneath the Martian surface. The microprobes will test the ability of very small spacecraft to deploy future instruments for soil sampling, meteorology and seismic monitoring. A key instrument will draw a tiny soil sample into a chamber, heat it and use a miniature laser to look for signs of vaporized water ice.

Also onboard the lander is a light detection and ranging (LIDAR) experiment provided by Russia's Space Research Institute. The instrument will detect and determine the altitude of atmospheric dust hazes and ice clouds above the lander. Inside the instrument is a small microphone, furnished by the Planetary Society, Pasadena, California, which will record the sounds of wind gusts, blowing dust and mechanical operations onboard the spacecraft itself.

The lander is expected to operate on the surface for 60 to 90 Martian days through the planet's southern summer (a Martian day is 24 hours, 37 minutes). MPL will use the MGS as a data relay to Earth in place of the MCO. The mission will continue until the spacecraft can no longer protect itself from the cold and dark of lengthening nights and the return of the Martian seasonal polar frosts.

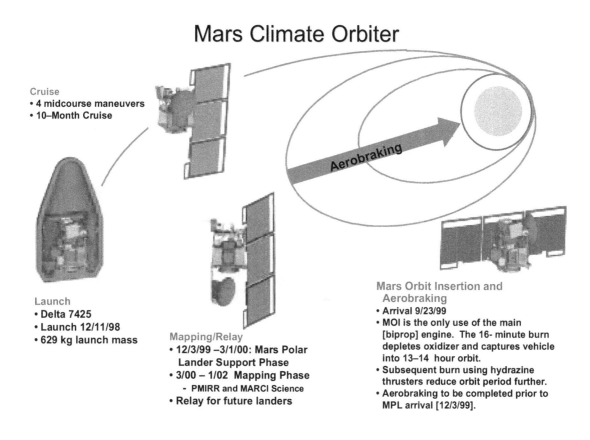

Figure 1

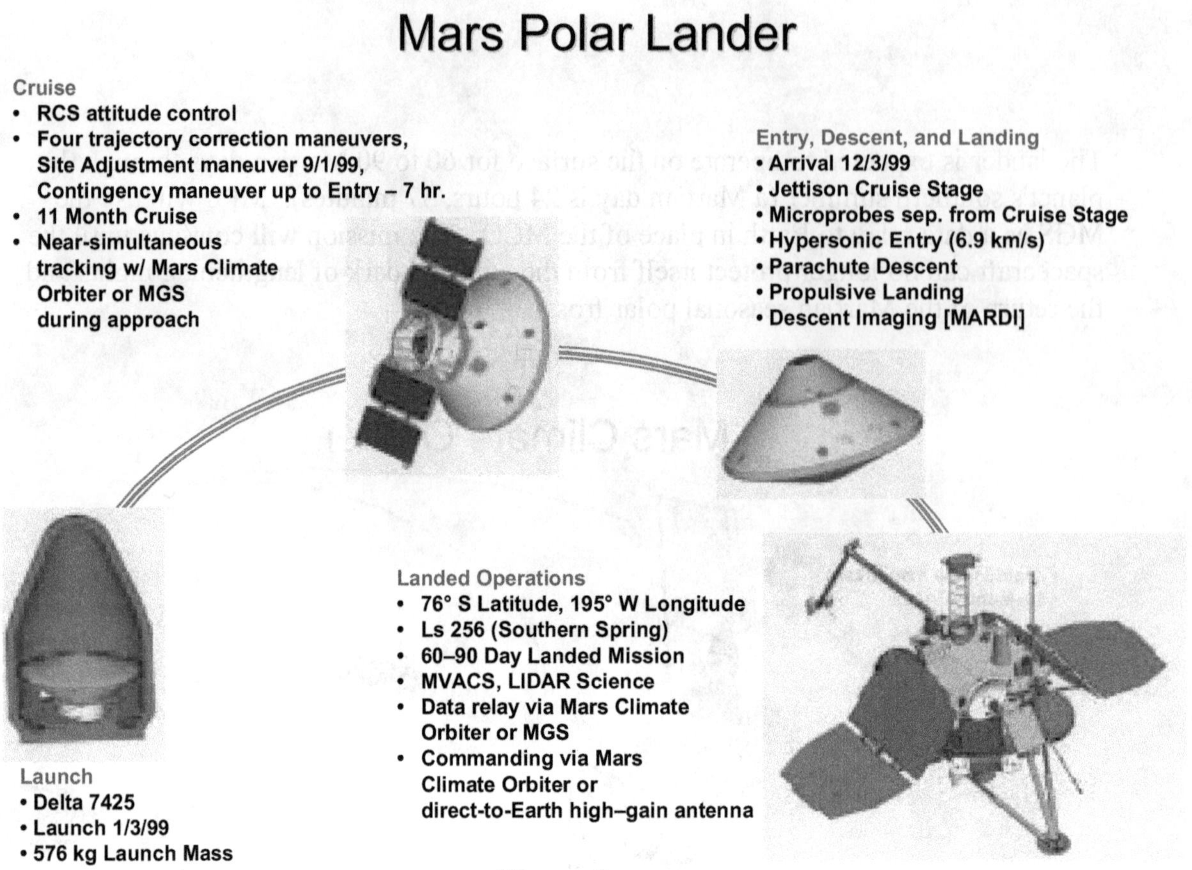

Mars Polar Lander

Cruise
- RCS attitude control
- Four trajectory correction maneuvers, Site Adjustment maneuver 9/1/99, Contingency maneuver up to Entry – 7 hr.
- 11 Month Cruise
- Near-simultaneous tracking w/ Mars Climate Orbiter or MGS during approach

Entry, Descent, and Landing
- Arrival 12/3/99
- Jettison Cruise Stage
- Microprobes sep. from Cruise Stage
- Hypersonic Entry (6.9 km/s)
- Parachute Descent
- Propulsive Landing
- Descent Imaging [MARDI]

Landed Operations
- 76° S Latitude, 195° W Longitude
- Ls 256 (Southern Spring)
- 60–90 Day Landed Mission
- MVACS, LIDAR Science
- Data relay via Mars Climate Orbiter or MGS
- Commanding via Mars Climate Orbiter or direct-to-Earth high–gain antenna

Launch
- Delta 7425
- Launch 1/3/99
- 576 kg Launch Mass

Figure 2

Entry/Descent/Landing Phase

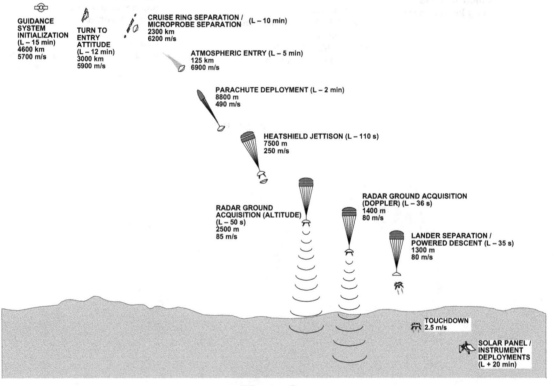

GUIDANCE SYSTEM INITIALIZATION (L – 15 min) 4600 km 5700 m/s

TURN TO ENTRY ATTITUDE (L – 12 min) 3000 km 5900 m/s

CRUISE RING SEPARATION / MICROPROBE SEPARATION (L – 10 min) 2300 km 6200 m/s

ATMOSPHERIC ENTRY (L – 5 min) 125 km 6900 m/s

PARACHUTE DEPLOYMENT (L – 2 min) 8800 m 490 m/s

HEATSHIELD JETTISON (L – 110 s) 7500 m 250 m/s

RADAR GROUND ACQUISITION (ALTITUDE) (L – 50 s) 2500 m 85 m/s

RADAR GROUND ACQUISITION (DOPPLER) (L – 36 s) 1400 m 80 m/s

LANDER SEPARATION / POWERED DESCENT (L – 35 s) 1300 m 80 m/s

TOUCHDOWN 2.5 m/s

SOLAR PANEL / INSTRUMENT DEPLOYMENTS (L + 20 min)

Figure 3

2. Mars Climate Orbiter (MCO) Mishap

The MCO had been on a trajectory toward Mars since its launch on December 11, 1998. All spacecraft systems had been performing nominally until an abrupt loss of mission shortly after the start of the Mars Orbit Insertion burn on September 23, 1999. Throughout spring and summer of 1999, concerns existed at the working level regarding discrepancies observed between navigation solutions. Residuals between the expected and observed Doppler signature of the more frequent AMD events was noted but only informally reported. As MCO approached Mars, three orbit determination schemes were employed. Doppler and range solutions were compared to those computed using only Doppler or range data. The Doppler-only solutions consistently indicated a flight path insertion closer to the planet. These discrepancies were not resolved.

On September 8,1999, the final planned interplanetary Trajectory Correction Maneuver-4 (TCM-4) was computed. This maneuver was expected to adjust the trajectory such that soon after the Mars orbital insertion (MOI) burn, the first periapse altitude (point of closest approach to the planet) would be at a distance of 226km. See figure 4. This would have also resulted in the second periapse altitude becoming 210km, which was desired for the subsequent MCO aerobraking phase. TCM-4 was executed as planned on September 15, 1999.

Mars orbit insertion was planned on September 23, 1999. During the weeklong timeframe between TCM-4 and MOI, orbit determination processing by the operations navigation team indicated that the first periapse distance had decreased to the range of 150-170km

During the 24 hours preceding MOI, MCO began to feel the strong effects of Mar's gravitational field and tracking data was collected to measure this and incorporate it into the orbit determination process. Approximately one hour prior to MOI, processing of this more accurate tracking data was completed. Based on this data, the first periapse altitude was calculated to be as low as 110km. The minimum periapse altitude considered survivable by MCO is 80 km.

The MOI engine start occurred at 09:00:46 (UTC) on September 23, 1999. All systems performed nominally until Mars's occultation loss of signal at 09:04:52 (UTC), which occurred 49 seconds earlier than predicted. Signal was not reacquired following the 21 minute predicted occultation interval. Exhaustive attempts to reacquire signal continued through September 25, 1999, but were unsuccessful.

On September 27, 1999, the operations navigation team consulted with the spacecraft engineers to discuss navigation discrepancies regarding velocity change (ΔV) modeling issues. On September 29, 1999, it was discovered that the small forces ΔV's reported by the spacecraft engineers for use in orbit determination solutions was low by a factor of 4.45 (1 pound force=4.45 Newtons) because the impulse bit data contained in the AMD file was delivered in lb-sec instead of the specified and expected units of Newton-sec.

Finally, after the fact navigation estimates, using all available data through loss of signal, with corrected values for the small forces ΔV's, indicated an initial periapsis (lowest point of orbit) of 57 km which was judged too low for spacecraft survival.

Schematic MCO Encounter Diagram
Not to scale

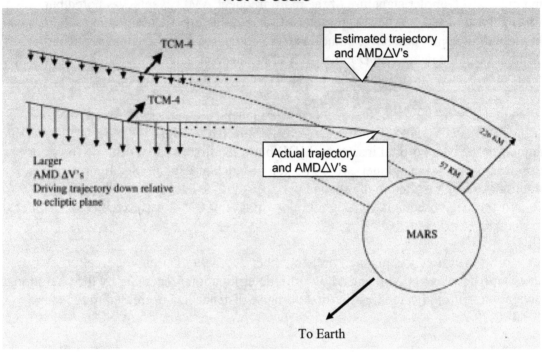

Figure 4

3. Method of Investigation

On October 15, 1999, the Associate Administrator for Space Science established the NASA MCO Mishap Investigation Board (MIB), with Art Stephenson, Director of Marshall Space Flight Center, Chairman. The Phase I MIB activity, reported herein, addresses paragraph 4.A, of the letter establishing the MCO MIB (Appendix). Specifically, paragraph 4.A. requests that the MIB focus on any aspects of the MCO mishap which must be addressed in order to contribute to the Mars Polar Lander's safe landing on Mars.

The Phase I Mishap Investigation Board meetings were conducted at the Jet Propulsion Lab (JPL) on October 18-22. Members of the JPL/Lockheed Martin Astronautics team provided an overview of the MCO spacecraft, operations, navigation plan, and the software validation process. The discussion was allowed to transition to any subject the Board deemed important, so that many issues were covered in great depth in these briefings.

Briefings were also held on the MPL systems, with emphasis on the interplanetary trajectory control and the Entry, Descent, and Landing aspects of the mission. The Board also sent a member to participate in MPL's critical event review for Entry, Descent, and Landing (EDL) held at LMA Denver on October 21. Several substantial findings were brought back from this review and incorporated into the Board's findings. A focused splinter meeting was held with the Board's navigation experts and the JPL navigation team on MCO and MPL questions and concerns. Splinter meetings were also held with the JPL and LMA propulsion teams and with the JPL MSP'98 project scientists.

Prior to the establishment of the MCO MIB, two investigative boards had been established by JPL. Both the Navigation Failure Assessment Team and the JPL Mishap Investigation Board presented their draft findings to the MCO Board.

The root cause, contributing causes and observations were determined by the Board through a process that alternated between individual brainstorming and group discussion. In addition, the Board developed MPL observations and recommendations not directly related to the MCO mishap.

A number of contributing causes were identified as well as number of observations. The focus of these contributing causes and observations were on those that could impact the MPL. Recommendations for the MPL were developed and are presented in this Phase I report. Recommendations regarding changing the NASA program processes to prevent a similar failure in the future are the subject of the Phase II portion of the Board's activity as described in Section 8 of this report.

The MPL observations contained in this report refer to conditions as of October 22, 1999, and do not reflect actions taken subsequent to that date.

4. Mars Climate Orbiter (MCO) Root Cause and Mars Polar Lander (MPL) Recommendations

During the mishap investigation process, specific policy is in-place to conduct the investigation and to provide key definitions to guide the investigation. NASA Procedures and Guidelines (NPG) 8621 Draft 1, "NASA Procedures and Guidelines for Mishap Reporting, Investigating, and Recordkeeping" provides these key definitions for NASA mishap investigations. NPG 8621 (Draft 1) defines a root cause as: "Along a chain of events leading to a mishap, the first causal action or failure to act that could have been controlled systematically either by policy/practice/procedure or individual adherence to policy/practice/procedure". Based on this definition, the Board determined that there was one root cause for the MCO mishap.

MCO Root Cause

The MCO MIB has determined that the root cause for the loss of the MCO spacecraft was the failure to use metric units in the coding of a ground software file, "Small Forces," used in trajectory models. Specifically, thruster performance data in English units instead of metric units was used in the software application code titled SM_FORCES (small forces). The output from the SM_FORCES application code as required by a MSOP Project Software Interface Specification (SIS) was to be in metric units of Newton-seconds (N-s). Instead, the data was reported in English units of pound-seconds (lbf-s). The Angular Momentum Desaturation (AMD) file contained the output data from the SM_FORCES software. The SIS, which was not followed, defines both the format and units of the AMD file generated by ground-based computers. Subsequent processing of the data from AMD file by the navigation software algorithm therefore, underestimated the effect on the spacecraft trajectory by a factor of 4.45, which is the required conversion factor from force in pounds to Newtons. An erroneous trajectory was computed using this incorrect data.

MPL Recommendations:

The Board recommends that the MPL project verify the consistent use of units throughout the MPL spacecraft design and operation. The Board recommends a software audit for SIS compliance on all data transferred between the JPL operations navigation team and the spacecraft operations team.

5. Mars Climate Orbiter (MCO) Contributing Causes and Mars Polar Lander (MPL) Recommendations

Section 6 of NPG 8621 (Draft 1) provides key definitions for NASA mishap investigations. NPG 8621 (Draft 1) defines a contributing cause as: "A factor, event or circumstance which led directly or indirectly to the dominant root cause, or which contributed to the severity of the mishap. Based on this definition, the Board determined that there were 8 contributing causes that relate to recommendations for the Mars Polar Lander.

MCO Contributing Cause No. 1: Modeling of Spacecraft Velocity Changes

Angular momentum management is required to keep the spacecraft's reaction wheels (or flywheels) within their linear (unsaturated) range. This is accomplished through thruster firings using a procedure called Angular Momentum Desaturation (AMD). When an AMD event occurs, relevant spacecraft data is telemetered to the ground, processed by the SM_FORCES software, and placed into a file called the Angular Momentum Desaturation (AMD) file. The JPL operations navigation team used data derived from the Angular Momentum Desaturation (AMD) file to model the forces on the spacecraft resulting from these specific thruster firings. Modeling of these small forces is critical for accurately determining the spacecraft's trajectory. Immediately after the thruster firing, the velocity change (ΔV) is computed using an impulse bit and thruster firing time for each of the thrusters. The impulse bit models the thruster performance provided by the thruster manufacturer. The calculation of the thruster performance is carried out both on-board the spacecraft and on ground support system computers. Mismodeling only occurred in the ground software.

The Software Interface Specification (SIS), used to define the format of the AMD file, specifies the units associated with the impulse bit to be Newton-seconds (N-s). Newton-seconds are the proper units for impulse (Force x Time) for metric units. The AMD software installed on the spacecraft used metric units for the computation and was correct. In the case of the ground software, the impulse bit reported to the AMD file was in English units of pounds (force)-seconds (lbf-s) rather than the metric units specified. Subsequent processing of the impulse bit values from the AMD file by the navigation software underestimated the effect of the thruster firings on the spacecraft trajectory by a factor of 4.45 (1 pound force=4.45 Newtons).

During the first four months of the MCO cruise flight, the ground software AMD files were not used in the orbit determination process because of multiple file format errors and incorrect quaternion (spacecraft attitude data) specifications. Instead, the operations navigation team used email from the contractor to notify them when an AMD desaturation event was occurring, and they attempted to model trajectory perturbations on their own, based on this timing information. Four months were used to fix the file problems and it was not until April 1999 that the operations team could begin using the correctly formatted files. Almost immediately (within a week) it became apparent that the files contained anomalous data that was indicating underestimation of the trajectory perturbations due to desaturation events. These file format and content errors early in the cruise mission contributed to the operations navigation team not being able to quickly detect and investigate what would become the root cause.

In April 1999, it became apparent that there was some type of mismodeling of the AMD maneuvers. In attempting to resolve this anomaly, two factors influenced the investigation. First, there was limited observability of the total magnitude of the thrust because of the relative geometry of the thrusters used for AMD activities and the Earth-to-spacecraft line of sight. The navigation team can only directly observe the thrust effects along the line of sight using the measurements of the spacecraft's Doppler shift. In the case of Mars Climate Orbiter (MCO), the major component of thrust during an AMD event was perpendicular to the line-of-sight. The limited observability of the direct effect of the thruster activity meant a systematic error due to the incorrect modeling of the thruster effects was present but undetected in the trajectory estimation. Second, the primary component of the thrust was also perpendicular to the spacecraft's flight path. See figure 4. In the case of MCO, this perturbation to the trajectory resulted in the actual spacecraft trajectory at the closest approach to Mars being lower than what was estimated by the navigators.

MPL Recommendation:

The Board recommends that the small forces models used for MPL be validated to assure the proper treatment of the modeled forces, including thruster activity used for attitude control and solar radiation pressure. Additionally, several other navigation methods should be compared to the prime navigation method to help uncover any mismodeled small forces on MPL

Mars Climate Orbiter (MCO) Contributing Cause No. 2: Knowledge of Spacecraft Characteristics

The operations navigation team was not intimately familiar with the attitude operations of the spacecraft, especially with regard to the MCO attitude control system and related subsystem parameters. This unfamiliarity caused the operations navigation team to perform increased navigation analysis to quantify an orbit determination residual error. The error was masked by the lack of information regarding the actual velocity change (ΔV) imparted by the angular momentum desaturation (AMD) events. A line of sight error was detectable in the processing of the tracking measurement data, but its significance was not fully understood. Additionally, a separate navigation team was used for the MCO development and test phase. The operations navigation team came onboard shortly before launch and did not participate in any of the testing of the ground software. The operations navigation team also did not participate in the Preliminary Design review nor in the critical design review process. Critical information on the control and desaturation of the MCO momentum was not passed on to the operations navigation team.

MPL Recommendation:

The Board recommends that the MPL operations navigation team be provided with additional training and specific information regarding the attitude subsystems and any other subsystem which may have an impact on the accuracy of navigation solutions. To facilitate this, a series face-to-face meetings should be conducted with the spacecraft development, and operations teams to disseminate updated information and to discuss anomalies from this point forward. Long-term onsite support of an LMA articulation and attitude control system (AACS) person should be provided to the operations navigation team or a JPL resident AACS expert should be brought on the team to help facilitate better communication.

MCO Contributing Cause No. 3: Trajectory Correction Maneuver (TCM-5)

During the MCO approach, a contingency maneuver plan was in place to execute an MCO Trajectory Correction Maneuver (TCM) -5 to raise the <u>second</u> periapsis passage of the MCO to a safe altitude. For a low initial periapsis, TCM-5 could also have been used shortly before the Mars Orbit Insertion (MOI) as an emergency maneuver to attain a safer altitude. A request to perform a TCM-5 was discussed verbally shortly before the MOI onboard procedure was initiated, but was never executed.

Several concerns prevented the operations team from implementing TCM-5. Analysis, tests, and procedures to commit to a TCM-5 in the event of a safety issue were not completed, nor attempted. Therefore, the operations team was not prepared for such a maneuver. Also, TCM-5 was not executed because the MOI maneuver timeline onboard the spacecraft took priority. This onboard procedure did not allow time for the upload, execution, and navigation verification of such a maneuver. Additionally, any change to the baselined orbit scenario could have exceeded the time for the MCO aerobraking phase when MCO was needed to support the communications of the MPL spacecraft. The criticality to perform TCM-5 was not fully understood by the spacecraft operations or operations navigation personnel.

The MPL mission sequence also contains a 'contingency' TCM-5 for a final correction of the incoming trajectory to meet the entry target conditions for the MPL Entry, Descent, and Landing (EDL) phase. The MPL TCM-5 is currently listed as a contingency maneuver. This TCM-5 also has not been explicitly determined as a required maneuver and there is still confusion over the necessity and the scheduling of it.

MPL Recommendation:

The board recommends that the operations team adequately prepare for the possibility of executing TCM-5. Maneuver planning and scheduling should be baselined as well as specific criteria for deciding whether or not the maneuver should be executed. The full operations team should be briefed on the TCM-5 maneuver execution scenario and should be fully trained and prepared for its execution. If possible, an integrated simulation of the maneuver computations, validation, and uplink should be performed to verify team readiness and sufficient time scheduling. Additionally, a TCM-5 lead should be appointed to develop the process for the execution and testing of the maneuver and to address the multiple decision process of performing TCM-5 with respect to the EDL.

MCO Contributing Cause No. 4: Systems Engineering Process

One of the problems observed by the Board on MCO was that the systems engineering process did not adequately transition from development to operations. There were a number of opportunities for the systems engineering organization to identify the units problem leading to mission loss of MCO.. The lack of an adequate systems engineering function contributed to the lack of understanding on the part of the navigation team of essential spacecraft design characteristics and the spacecraft team understanding of the navigation challenge. It also resulted in inadequate contingency preparation process to address unpredicted performance during operations, a lack of understanding of several critical operations tradeoffs, and it exacerbated the communications difficulties between the subsystem engineers (e.g navigation, AACS, propulsion).

For example, the Angular Momentum Desaturation (AMD) events on MCO occurred 10-14 times more often than was expected by the operations navigation team. This was because the MCO solar array was asymmetrical relative to the spacecraft body as compared to Mars Global Surveyor which had symmetrical solar arrays. This asymmetric effect significantly increased the Sun-induced (solar pressure-induced) momentum buildup on the spacecraft. To minimize this effect, a daily $180°$ flip was baselined to cancel the angular momentum build up. Systems engineering trade studies performed later determined that this so-called "barbecue" mode was not needed and it was deleted from the spacecraft operations plan. Unfortunately, these systems engineering decisions and their impact to the spacecraft and the spacecraft trajectory were not communicated to the operations navigation team. The increased AMD events resulting from this decision coupled with the fact that the angular momentum (impulse) data was in English, rather than metric, units contributed to the MCO mission failure.

MPL Recommendation:

The Board recommends that the MPL project establish and fully staff a systems engineering organization with roles and responsibilities defined. This team should concentrate on the TCM-5 and EDL activities. They should support updating MPL risk assessments for both EDL and Mars ground operations, and review the systems engineering on the entire MPL mission to ensure that the MPL mission is ready for the EDL sequence.

MCO Contributing Cause No. 5: Communications Among Project Elements

In the MCO project, and again in the MPL project, there is evidence of inadequate communications between the project elements, including the development and operations teams, the operations navigation and operations teams, the project management and technical teams, and the project and technical line management.

It was clear that the operations navigation team did not communicate their trajectory concerns effectively to the spacecraft operations team or project management. In addition, the spacecraft operations team did not understand the concerns of the operations navigation team. The Board found the operations navigation team supporting MCO to be somewhat isolated from the MCO development and operations teams, as well as from its own line organization, by inadequate communication. One contributing factor to this lack of communication may have been the operations navigation team's assumption that MCO had Mars Global Surveyor (MGS) heritage and the resulting expectation that much of the MCO hardware and software was similar to that on MGS. This apparently caused the operations navigation team to acquire insufficient technical knowledge of the spacecraft, its operation, and its potential impact to navigation computations. For example, the operations navigation team did not know until long after launch that the spacecraft routinely calculated, and transmitted to Earth, velocity change data for the angular momentum desaturation events. An early comparison of these spacecraft-generated data with the tracking data might have uncovered the units problem that ultimately led to the loss of the spacecraft. When conflicts in the data were uncovered, the team relied on e-mail to solve problems, instead of formal problem resolution processes such as the Incident, Surprise, Anomaly (ISA) reporting procedure. Failing to adequately employ the problem tracking system contributed to this problem "slipping through the cracks."

A splinter meeting between some members of the Board and the operations navigation team illustrated the fact that there was inadequate communication between the operations navigation team and mission operations teams. While the Board was notified of potential changes in the MPL landing site, it was discovered that this knowledge was not fully conveyed to the entire MPL operations navigation team. Inadequate systems engineering support exacerbated the isolation of the navigation team. A robust system's engineering team could have helped improve communication between the operations navigation team and other, navigation critical subsystems (e.g. propulsion, AACS). Systems engineering support would have enhanced the operations navigation team's abilities to reach critical decisions and would have provided oversight in navigation mission assurance.

The operations navigation team could have benefited from independent peer reviews to validate their navigation analysis technique and to provide independent oversight of the trajectory analyses.

Defensive mechanisms have also developed between the team members on MPL as a result of the MCO failure. This is causing inadequate communication across project elements and a failure to elevate concerns with full end-to-end problem ownership.

MPL Recommendations:

The board recommends that the MPL project should stress to the project staff that communication is critical and empower team members to forcefully elevate any issue, keeping the originator in the loop through formal closure. Project management should establish a policy and communicate it to all team members that they are empowered to forcefully and vigorously elevate concerns as high, either vertically or horizontally in the organization, as necessary to get attention. This policy should be constantly reinforced as a means for mission success.

The MPL project should increase the amount of formal and informal face-to-face communications with all team elements including science, navigation, propulsion, etc. and especially for those elements that have critical interfaces like navigation and spacecraft guidance and control. (e.g. co-location of a navigation team member with the spacecraft guidance and control group).

The project should establish a routine forum for informal communication between all team members at the same time so everyone can hear what is happening. (e.g. a 15 minute stand-up tag-up meeting every morning).

The project and JPL management should encourage the MPL team to be skeptics and raise all concerns. All members of the MPL team should take concerns personally and see that they receive closure no matter what it takes.

The operations navigation team should implement and conduct a series of independent peer reviews in sufficient time to support MPL mission critical navigation events.

The Board also recommends that the MPL project assign a mission systems engineer as soon as possible. This mission systems engineer would provide the systems engineering bridge between the spacecraft system, the instrument system and the ground/operations system to maximize the probability of mission success.

MCO Contributing Cause No. 6: Operations Navigation Team Staffing

The Board found that the staffing of the operations navigation team was less than adequate. During the time leading up to the loss of the MCO, the Mars Surveyor

Operations Project (MSOP) was running 3 missions simultaneously (MGS, MCO, MPL). This tended to dilute the focus on any one mission, such as MCO. During the time before Mars orbit insertion (MOI), MCO navigation was handled by the navigation team lead and the MCO navigator. Due to the loss of MCO, MPL is to have three navigators, but only two were on-board at the time of the Board's meetings during the week of Oct. 18-22, 1999. The Board was told that 24 hour/day navigation staffing is planned for a brief period before MPL entry, descent, and landing (EDL). Such coverage may be difficult even for a team of three navigators and certainly was not possible for the single navigator of MCO.

MPL Recommendation:

The Board recommends that the operations navigation staff be augmented with experienced people to support the MPL EDL sequence. The MPL project should assign and train a third navigator to the operations team to support the EDL activities as soon as possible. In addition, the operations navigation team should identify backup personnel that could be made available to serve in some of the critical roles in the event that one of the key navigators becomes ill prior to the EDL activity.

The Board also recommends that the MPL project prepare contingency plans for backing up key personnel for mission-critical functions in any area of the Project.

MCO Contributing Cause No. 7: Training of Personnel

The Board found several instances of inadequate training in the MCO project. The operations navigation team had not received adequate training on the MCO spacecraft design and its operations. Some members of the MCO team did not recognize the purpose and the use of the ISA. The small forces software development team needed additional training in the ground software development process and in the use and importance of following the Mission Operations Software Interface Specification (SIS). There was inadequate training of the MCO team on the importance of an acceptable approach to end to end testing of the small forces ground software. There was also inadequate training on the recognition and treatment of mission critical small forces ground software.

MPL Recommendation:

The Board recommends that the MPL operations navigation team receive proper training in the spacecraft design and operations. Identify the MPL mission critical ground software and ensure that all such ground software meets the MPL software development plans. Ensure that the entire MPL team is trained on the ISA Process and its purpose-- emphasize a "Mission Safety First" attitude. Encourage any issue to be written up as an ISA. Review all current anomalies and generate appropriate ISAs.

MCO Contributing Cause No. 8: Verification and Validation Process

Several verification and validation process issues were uncovered during the Board's review of the MCO program that should be noted. The Software Interface Specification (SIS) was developed but not properly used in the small forces ground software development and testing. End-to-end testing to validate the small forces ground software performance and its applicability to the specification did not appear to be accomplished. It was not clear that the ground software independent verification and validation was accomplished for MCO. The interface control process and the verification of specific ground system interfaces was not completed or was completed with insufficient rigor.

MPL Recommendation:

The Board recommends that the MPL project develop a system verification matrix for all project requirements including all Interface Control Documents (ICDs). The MPL team should review the system verification matrix at all remaining major reviews. The MPL project should require end users at the technical level to sign off on the ground software applications and products and the MPL project should review all ground software applications, including all new and reused software packages for applicability and correct data transfer.

6. Mars Climate Orbiter (MCO) Observations and Recommendations

Section 6 of NPG 8621 (Draft 1) provides key definitions for NASA mishap investigations. NPG 8621 (Draft 1) defines a significant observation as: "A factor, event or circumstance identified during the investigation which was not contributing to the mishap, but if left uncorrected, has the potential to cause a mishap...or increase the severity should a mishap occur." Based on this definition, the Board determined that there were 10 observations that relate to recommendations for the MLP.

MCO Observation No. 1: Trajectory Margin for Mars Orbit Insertion

As the MCO proceeded through cruise phase for the subsequent MOI and aerobraking phases, the margins needed to ensure a successful orbit capture eroded over time. During the cruise phase and immediately preceding MOI, inadequate statistical analyses were employed to fully understand the dispersions of the trajectory and how these would impact the final MOI sequence. This resulted in a misunderstanding of the actual vehicle trajectory. As described previously, the actual trajectory path resulted in a periapsis much lower than expected. In addition, TCM-5 contingency plans, in the event of an anomaly, were not adequately worked out ahead of time. The absence of planning, tests, and commitment criteria for the execution of TCM-5 may have played a significant role in the decision to not change the MCO trajectory using the TCM-5 maneuver. The failure to execute TCM-5 is discussed as a contributing cause of the mishap. Spacecraft propellant reserves and schedule margins during the aerobraking phases were not used to mitigate the risk of uncertainties in the closest approach distance at MOI.

MPL Recommendations:

The Board recommends that the MPL project improve the data analysis procedures for fitting trajectory data to models, that they implement an independent navigation peer panel and navigation advisory group as a means to further validate the models to the trajectory data, and that they engage the entire MPL team in TCM and Entry, Descent, and Landing (EDL) planning.

MCO Observation No. 2: Independent Reviews

The Board noted that a number of reviews took place without the proper representation of key personnel; operations navigation personnel did not attend the spacecraft Preliminary and Critical Design Reviews. Attendance of these individuals may have allowed the flow of pertinent and applicable spacecraft characteristics to the operations navigation team.

Knowledge of these characteristics by the operations navigation may have helped them resolve the problem.

Key modeling issues were missed in the interpretation of trajectory data by the operations navigation team. The absence of a rigorous, independent navigation peer review process contributed to these issues being missed.

MPL Recommendations:

Provide for operations navigation discipline presence at major reviews. Ensure subsystem specialists attend major reviews and participate in transfer of lessons learned to the operations navigation team and others. Implement a formal peer review process on all mission critical events, especially critical navigation events.

MCO Observation No. 3: Contingency Planning Process

Inadequate contingency planning for TCM-5 was observed to play a part in the MCO failure. The MCO operational contingency plans for TCM-5 were not well defined and or completely understood by all team members on the MCO operational team.

The MCO project did not have a defined set of Go–No Go criteria for using TCM-5. There was no process in place to review the evaluation and decision criteria by the project and subsystem engineers before commitment to TCM-5. Polling of the team by the MCO Flight Operations Manager should establish a clear commitment from each subsystem lead that he or she has reviewed the appropriate data and believes that the spacecraft is in the proper configuration for the event.

MPL Recommendations:

Contingency plans need to be defined, the products associated with the contingencies fully developed, the contingency products tested and the operational team trained on the use of the contingency plans and on the use of the products. Since all possible contingency plans cannot be developed, a systematic assessment of all potential failure modes must be done as a basis for the development of the project contingency plans. The MPL team should establish a firm set of "Go no-go" criteria for each contingency scenario and the individual members of the operations team and subsystem experts should be polled prior to committing to the event.

MCO Observation No. 4: Transition from Development to Operations

The Board found that the overall project plan did not provide for a careful handover from the development project to the very busy operations project. MCO was the first JPL mission to transition a minimal number of the development team into a multi-mission operations team. Very few JPL personnel and no MCO navigation personnel, transitioned with the project. Furthermore, MCO was the first mission to be supported by the multi-mission MSOP team.

During the months leading up to MCO MOI, the MSOP team had some key personnel vacancies and a change in top management. The operations navigation personnel in MSOP were working MGS operations, which had experienced some in-flight anomalies. They were expecting MCO to closely resemble MGS. They had not been involved in the initial development of the navigation plan and did not show ownership of the plan, which had been handed off to them by the MCO development team. The MSOP had no systems engineering and no mission assurance personnel who might have acted as an additional set of eyes in the implementation of the process.

It should be noted that the MPL navigation development engineer did transition to operations.

MPL Recommendations:

Increase the MPL operations and operations navigation teams as appropriate. Augment the teams by recalling key members of the development team and specialists from the line organization. Consider more collocation of JPL/LMA personnel through EDL. Conduct a rigorous review of the handoff from the JPL operations navigation team to the LMA EDL team, particularly the ICD and all critical events.

MCO Observation No. 5: Matrix Management

The Board observed that line organizations, especially that of the operations navigation team, were not significantly engaged in project-related activity. In the case of navigation, the Board observed little evidence of contact between line supervision and navigators supporting the project.

MPL Recommendation:

Expeditiously involve line management in independently reviewing and following through the work remaining to achieve a successful MPL landing.

MCO Observation No. 6: Mission Assurance

The Board observed the absence of a mission assurance manager in MSOP. It was felt that such a presence earlier in the program might have helped to improve project communication, insure that project requirements were met. Items that the mission assurance manager could have addressed for MCO included ensuring that the AMD file met the requirements of the SIS and tracking ISA resolutions. The mission assurance manager would promote the healthy questioning of "what could go wrong." The Board explicitly heard an intention to fill the mission assurance position for MPL, but this had not happened as of October 22, 1999.

MPL Recommendation:

Assign a mission assurance manager in MSOP as soon as possible.

MCO Observation No. 7: Science Involvement

The paradigm for the Mars Surveyor program is a capabilities-driven mission in which all elements, including science, were traded to achieve project objectives within the overall constraints of cost and schedule. Success of such missions requires full involvement of the mission science personnel in the management process. In addition, science personnel with relevant expertise should be included in all decisions where expert knowledge of Mars is required. While this was generally the case for the Mars '98 program, such experts were not fully involved in the decisions not to perform TCM-5 prior to Mars orbit insertion.

MPL Recommendation:

Fully involve the Project Scientist in the management process for the remainder of the MPL mission, including decisions relating to Entry, Descent, and Landing.

MCO Observation No. 8: Navigation Capabilities

JPL's navigation of interplanetary spacecraft has worked well for 30 years. In the case of MCO there was a widespread perception that "Orbiting Mars is routine." This perception resulted in inadequate attention to navigation risk mitigation.

MPL Recommendation:

MPL project personnel should question and challenge everything—even those things that have always worked. JPL top management should provide the necessary emphasis to bring about a cultural change.

MCO Observation No. 9: Management of Critical Flight Decisions

During its deliberations, the Board observed significant uncertainty and discussions about such things as the project's plan for trajectory correction maneuvers (TCMs) and the planned primary and alternate landing sites for MPL. Planning for TCM 5 on MCO was inadequate. TCM 5 for MPL was still being described as a contingency maneuver during the Board's deliberations. The Board also notes evidence of delayed decisions at the October 21, 1999, MPL Critical Events Review for Entry, Descent, and Landing.

MPL Recommendation:

Require timely, disciplined decisions in planning and executing the remainder of the MPL mission.

MCO Observation No. 10:   Analyzing What Could Go Wrong

The Board observed what appeared to be the lack of systematic analyses of "what could go wrong" with the Mars '98 projects. For example, the Board observed no fault tree or other *a priori* analyses of what could go wrong with MCO or MPL.

MPL Recommendation:

Conduct a fault tree analysis for the remainder of the MPL mission; follow-up on the results. Consider using an external facilitator; e.g., from nuclear industry or academia, if the necessary expertise in the *a priori* use of fault tree analysis does not exist at JPL.

7. Mars Polar Lander (MPL) Observations and Recommendations

As part of the MCO Phase I activity, the Board developed eight MPL observations and recommendations not directly related to the MCO mishap.

MPL Observation No. 1: Use of Supplemental Tracking Data Types

The use of supplemental tracking data types to enhance or increase the accuracy of the MPL navigation solutions was discussed. One data type listed in the MPL Mission Planning Databook as a requirement to meet the Entry Descent Landing (EDL) target condition to a performance of better than 95 percent is the Near Simultaneous Tracking (NST). Additional data types discussed were the use of a three-way measurement and a difference range process. These data types would be used independently to assess the two-way coherent measurement data types (range and Doppler) baselined by the prime operations navigation team. During the presentations to the MIB, it was stated that the MPL navigation team lead would be involved in the detailed analysis of the NST data. The application of a NST data type is relatively new to the MPL mission navigation procedure. These data types have not been previously used for MCO or MPL navigation. The results of the new data types in addition to range and Doppler only-solutions could potentially add to the uncertainty of the best estimate of the trajectory at the EDL conditions.

MPL Recommendation:

Identify the requirement for the use of the NST, 3-way, and difference range. Determine if the EDL target conditions can be met without them. An independent team should be responsible for the processing and assessment of these alternative tracking schemes. A process should be developed to utilize these data types as a crosscheck of the current 2-way coherent method. Ensure that the NST process is streamlined and well understood as it is incorporated into the nominal operations. If NST is necessary, focus work so as to not affect other routine navigation operations.

MPL Observation No. 2: Star Camera Attitude Maneuver (SCAM)

Prior to Entry, Descent and Landing (EDL), a multi-hour attitude calibration is planned on MPL. This so-called Star Camera Attitude Maneuver (SCAM) will reorient the spacecraft to provide optimal observation of stars in the star camera. The purpose of this maneuver is to calibrate the gyro drift bias and determine the vehicle attitude to a level of performance necessary to initiate the EDL maneuver sequence. The specific attitude required to successfully perform the SCAM results in a loss of spacecraft telemetry due to the fact that the MPL antenna is pointed away from Earth. Currently, the exact timing of the planned SCAM activity has not been finalized.

MPL Recommendation:

The MPL flight operations team should establish definitive SCAM requirements, especially the attitude accuracy needed prior to EDL and the length of time that MPL is required in the SCAM attitude. Clear operations scenarios should be developed and specific contingency operations procedures should be developed.

MPL Observation No. 3: Verification and Validation (V&V) of Lander Entry State File

Although the board was informed that a plan existed, the final end-to-end verification and validation of the Entry-Descent-Landing operational procedures had not been completed when the Board reviewed the project. This cannot be completed until after the ground software has successfully completed acceptance testing. Moreover, the generation and subsequent use of the Lander Entry State File (LESF) has not been tested. The data in the LESF is used to update the onboard estimate of Mars-relative position and velocity just prior to entry interface. Apparently this is a relatively new procedure for JPL and thus should receive focused attention.

MPL Recommendation:

The Board recommends that the MPL team perform an end-to-end V&V test of EDL including use of the LESF. Coordinate transformations and related equations used in the generation of this file should be checked carefully. The end-to-end test should include simulated uplinks of the LESF to the spacecraft and propagation of the simulated state vector to landing in a 6 degree-of-freedom simulation like the Simulation Test Laboratory. It may be beneficial to test it more than once with perhaps different scenarios or uplinked state vectors. Related to this issue is the need to have a baselined spacecraft timeline especially when entry interface is approaching. Any spacecraft maneuvers, e.g., SCAM maneuvers, from shortly before uplink of the LESF until entry interface need to be well-planned ahead of time, i.e., modeled by the navigators, so that the onboard navigation state at entry interface will be as accurate as possible.

If possible, provide for the capability to use a preliminary navigation solution for EDL navigation initialization in case of a temporary uplink problem, i.e., uplink an LESF file before it is really needed so that if an anomaly occurs in that process, the onboard EDL navigation system will have something reasonable to work with, albeit perhaps not as accurate as desired.

MPL Observation No. 4: Roles and Responsibilities of Individuals

In the wake of the MCO loss and the subsequent augmentation of the MPL team, the Board observed that roles and responsibilities of some individuals in MSOP are unclear. A recurring theme in the Board's deliberations was one of "Who's in charge?" Another such recurring theme was one of "Who's the mission manager?" The Board perceived hesitancy and wavering on the part of people attempting to answer this question. One answer was that the Flight Operations Manager (FOM) was acting like a mission manager, but is not actually designated as such.

MPL Recommendation:

The Board recommends that the MPL project clarify roles and responsibilities for all individuals on the team. Assign a person the role of mission manager for MPL and ensure that the entire team understands the leadership role that this person is empowered to provide to the MPL team.

MPL Observation No. 5: Cold Firing of Thrusters

Hydrazine has physical properties that are very similar to water. Hydrazine is a monopropellant that will be used in thrusters to slow the MPL spacecraft from about 75-80 meters/second to its landing velocity around 2.5 meters/second. This is accomplished by simultaneously pulse mode firing twelve (12) parallel catalytic thrusters. The key concern is the freezing point of hydrazine. Hydrazine freezes around 1 to 2° C, depending on the exact environmental conditions and hydrazine's purity. Furthermore, the spontaneous catalyst (i.e., initiates hydrazine decomposition at "room temperature)" used in all thrusters flying today, loses spontaneous reactivity as the catalyst bed temperature is lowered below 7°C. If the catalyst bed is very cold (i.e. well below 0° C), then there will be long ignition delays when the thrusters are commanded to fire. The results of these extremely cold and long ignition delay firings could produce high-pressure spikes and even possibly detonations. As a minimum, the cold catalyst bed induced ignition delays and the resulting irregular, pulses on startup, could seriously impact MPL dynamics and potentially the stability of the vehicle during the terminal descent operations, possibly leading to a non-upright touchdown.

Additional concern exists as to when the EDL operations team plans to turn on the heaters on the propellant lines feeding the hydrazine thrusters. The outer lines and the thrusters will have been cold "soaking" during the 11-month trip to Mars. If any of these lines are cold enough (well below 0°C), then the hydrazine might freeze when bled into the thruster valves. If this occurs, then there will be no impulse when the thrusters are commanded to fire.

It was stated by the project operations manager that all 12 thrusters (operating at 267 Newtons each) must all operate as commanded. Therefore, the above described thermal deficiencies should be a major concern for the MPL project team.

MPL Recommendations

The Board recommends that the MPL team examine the thermal analysis and determine when the heaters on the lines feeding the thrusters should be turned on to ensure adequate, stable liquid flow with sufficient positive margins. The Board also suggests that the MPL team should consider the use of very short catalyst bed thermal preconditioning pulses during lander propulsion system utilization (i.e., startup) to insure uniform pulse firing during terminal descent.

MPL Observation No. 6: MPL Terminal Descent Maneuver

The MPL terminal descent maneuver will use simultaneous soft pulse mode firings of 12 monopropellant hydrazine thrusters operating at 267 Newtons of thrust each. All these thrusters must operate in unison to ensure a stable descent. This type of powered descent maneuver has always been considered to be very difficult and stressing for a planetary exploration soft landing. Hence, in the last 35 years of planetary exploration, MPL is the first user of this soft pulsed thrust soft landing technique.

The concern has been that the feedline hydraulics and water hammer effects could be very complex and interactive. This issue could be further aggravated by fuel slosh, uneven feeding of propellant from the two tanks and possible center of gravity mismatch on the vehicle. Additional complications could result from non-uniform exhaust plume impingement on the lander legs sticking below the thruster nozzles due to any uneven pulse firings.

It should be recognized that under extreme worst case conditions for feedline interactions, it is possible that some thrusters could produce near zero thrust and some could produce nearly twice the expected thrust when commanded to operate.

MPL Recommendation:

It was stated many times by the MPL project team during the reviews with the Board, that a vast number of simulations, analyses and rigorous realistic tests were all carefully conducted during the development program to account for all these factors during the propulsive landing maneuver.

However, because of the extreme complexity of this landing maneuver, the EDL team should carefully re-verify that all the above described possible effects have been accounted for in the terminal maneuver strategies and control laws and the associated software for EDL operations.

MPL Observation No. 7: Decision Making Process

Discussions with MPL team members revealed uncertainty about mission-critical decisions that inhibited them from doing their job in a timely manner. The Board observed that there was discussion about the landing site for MPL at the time of our meetings at JPL. According to plan, there was consideration of moving to the backup site based on new information from MGS regarding landing site characteristics. Some elements of the Project team, e.g., some members of the operations navigation team, were not informed of this new information or the fact that the landing site was being reconsidered. There also was apparently uncertainty about the process for addressing this time-critical decision and about when it would be made.

MPL Recommendation:

Communicate widely the need for timely decisions that enable the various elements of the Project to perform their jobs. Establish a formal decision need-date tracking system that is communicated to the entire team. This system would identify the latest decision need date and the impact of not making the decision. All elements of the Project should provide input for establishing these dates and be informed of the decision schedules.

Assign an overall Mission Manager responsible for the success of the entire mission from spacecraft health to receipt of successful science data.

MPL Observation No. 8: Lander Science

The Board was informed that preparations for the Lander science program were in an incomplete state at the time of the Board's meeting due to the impacts resulting from the loss of the MCO. The redirection of resources due mainly to the loss of MCO caused the science team to become further behind in preparation for MPL science operations. Since the landed science program is limited to about three months by the short summer season near the Martian South Pole, maximum science return requires full readiness for science operations prior to EDL. Several additional managers were being assigned to address preparations for the science program.

MPL Recommendation:

Ensure that a detailed Lander science plan, tools, and necessary support are in place before the landing. The Project Scientist should be fully involved in the management of the science operations planning and implementation.

8. Phase II Plan

During the Phase II activity, the Board will review and evaluate the processes used by the MCO and MPL missions and other past mission successes and failures, develop lessons learned, make recommendations for future missions, and deliver a report no later than February 1, 2000. This report will cover the following topics and any other items the Board feels relevant as part of the investigation process.

1. Processes to detect, articulate, interpret and correct errors to ensure mission safety and reliability
2. Systems engineering issues, including, but not limited to:
   - Processes to identify primary mission success criteria as weighted against potential mission risks
   - Operational processes for data validation
   - Management structure and processes to enable error-free communications and procedure documentation
   - Processes to ensure that established procedures were followed
3. Testing, simulation and verification of missions operations
4. Work Force Development
5. Workforce culture: confidence or concern?
6. Independent assessments
7. Planetary Navigation Strategies: Ground and Autonomous
   - Accuracy & Precision that can be delivered
   - Current & future technologies to support Mars missions
   - Navigation requirements and pre-flight documentation

During the Phase II investigation process, the Board will obtain and analyze whatever evidence, facts, and opinions it considers relevant. It will use reports of studies, findings, recommendations, and other actions by NASA officials and contractors. The Board may conduct inquiries, hearings, tests, and other actions it deems appropriate. They will develop recommendations for preventive and other appropriate actions. Findings may warrant one or more recommendations, or they may stand-alone. The requirements in the NASA Policy Document (NPD) 8621.1G and NASA Procedures and Guidelines (NPG) 8621.1 (draft) will be followed for procedures, format, and the approval process.

Appendix

Letter Establishing the Mars Climate Orbiter Mishap Investigation Board

SD

TO: Distribution

FROM: S/Associate Administrator for Space Science

*SUBJECT: Establishment of the Mars Climate Orbiter (MCO) Mission
              Failure Mishap Investigation Board*

1.   INTRODUCTION/BACKGROUND

*The MCO spacecraft, designed to study the weather and climate of
Mars, was launched by a Delta rocket on December 11, 1998, from
Cape Canaveral Air Station, Florida. After cruise to Mars of
approximately 9 1/2 months, the spacecraft fired its main engine
to go into orbit around Mars at around 2 a.m. PDT on September 23,
1999.*

*Five minutes into the planned 16-minute burn, the spacecraft
passed behind the planet as seen from Earth. Signal reacquisition,
nominally expected at approximately 2:26 a.m. PDT when the
spacecraft was to reemerge from behind Mars, did not occur.
Fearing that a safehold condition may have been triggered on the
spacecraft, flight controllers at NASA's Jet Propulsion Laboratory
(JPL) in Pasadena, California, and at Lockheed Martin Astronautics
See figure 1. The spacecraft was to then skim through Mars' upper
atmosphere for several weeks in a*

*Efforts to find and communicate with MCO continued up until 3 p.m.
PDT on September 24, 1999, when they were abandoned. A
contingency was declared by MCO Program Executive,
Mr. Steve Brody at 3 p.m. EDT on September 24, 1999.*

2.   PURPOSE

*This establishes the NASA MCO Mission Failure Mishap Investigation
Board and sets forth its terms of reference, responsibilities, and
membership in accordance with NASA Policy Directive (NPD) 8621.1G.*

3.   ESTABLISHMENT

*a.   The MCO Mission Failure Mishap Investigation Board
(hereinafter called the Board) is hereby established in the
public's interest to gather information, analyze, and determine
the facts, as well as the actual or probable cause(s) of the MCO
Mission Failure Mishap in terms of (1) dominant root cause(s), (2)
contributing cause(s), and (3) significant observations and to
recommend preventive measures and other appropriate actions to
preclude recurrence of a similar mishap.*

*b.   The chairperson of the board will report to the NASA Office of
Space Science (OSS) Associate Administrator (AA) who is the
appointing official.*

4.   OBJECTIVES

*A.   An immediate priority for NASA is the safe landing on December 3,
1999, of the Mars Polar Lander (MPL) spacecraft, currently en
route to Mars. This investigation will be conducted recognizing*

the time-criticality of the MPL landing and the activities the MPL mission team must perform to successfully land the MPL spacecraft on Mars. Hence, the Board must focus first on any lessons learned of the MCO mission failure in order to help assure MPL's safe landing on Mars. The Board must deliver this report no later than November 5, 1999.

> i. The Board will recommend tests, analyses, and simulations capable of being conducted in the near term to prevent possible MPL failures and enable timely corrective actions.

> ii. The Board will review the MPL contingency plans and recommend improvements where possible.

B. The Board will review and evaluate all the processes used by the MCO mission, develop lessons learned, make recommendations for future missions, and deliver a final mishap investigation report no later than February 1, 2000. This report will cover the following topics and any other items the Board thinks relevant.

> i. Processes used to ensure mission safety and reliability with mission success as the primary objective. This will include those processes that do not just react to hard failures, but identify potential failures throughout the life of the mission for which corrective actions can be taken. It will also include asking if NASA has the correct philosophy for mission assurance in its space missions. That is:

> a) "Why should it fly?" versus "why it should not fly?",
> b) mission safety should not be compromised by cost and performance, and
> c) definition of adequacy, robustness, and margins-of-safety as applied to clearly defined mission success criteria.

> ii. Systems engineering issues, including, but not limited to:

> a) Processes to identify primary mission success criteria as weighted against potential mission risks,
> b) operational processes for data validation,
> c) Management structure and processes to enable error-free communications and procedure documentation, and
> d) processes to ensure that established procedures were followed.

> iii. Testing, simulation and verification of missions operations:

> a) What is the appropriate philosophy for conducting end-to-end simulations prior to flight?
> b) How much time and resources are appropriate for program planning?
> c) What tools should be developed and used routinely?
> d) How should operational and failure mode identification teams be formed and managed (teams that postulate failure modes and inspire in-depth review)?
> e) What are the success criteria for the mission, and what is required for operational team readiness prior to the Flight Readiness Review (i.e., test system tolerance to human and machine failure)?, and
> f) What is the recommended developmental process to ensure the operations team runs as many failure modes as possible prior to launch?

iv.   Personnel training provided to the MCO operations team, and assess its adequacy for conducting operations.

v.   Suggest specific recommendations to prevent basic types of human and machine error that may have led to the MCO failure.

vi.   Reexamine the current approach to planetary navigation. Specifically, are we asking for more accuracy and precision than we can deliver?

vii.   How in-flight accumulated knowledge was captured and utilized for future operational maneuvers.

5.   **AUTHORITIES AND RESPONSIBILITIES**

a.   *The Board will:*

1)   Obtain and analyze whatever evidence, facts, and opinions it considers relevant.   It will use reports of studies, findings, recommendations, and other actions by NASA officials and contractors.   The Board may conduct inquiries, hearings, tests, and other actions it deems appropriate.   It may take testimony and receive statements from witnesses.

2)   Determine the actual or probable cause(s) of the MCO mission failure, and document and prioritize their findings in terms of (a) the dominant root cause(s) of the mishap, (b) contributing cause(s), and (c) significant observation(s).   Pertinent observations may also be made.

3)   Develop recommendations for preventive and other appropriate actions.   A finding may warrant one or more recommendations, or it may stand-alone.

4)   Provide to the appointing authority, (a) periodic interim reports as requested by said authority, (b) a report by November 5, 1999, of those findings and recommendations and lessons learned necessary for consideration in preparation for the MPL landing, and (c) a final written report by February 1, 2000.   The requirements in the NPD 8621.1G and NASA Procedures and Guidelines (NPG) 8621.1 (draft) will be followed for procedures, format, and the approval process.

b.   *The Chairperson will:*

1)   Conduct Board activities in accordance with the provisions of NPD 8621.1G and NPG 8621.1 (draft) and any other instructions that the appointing authority may issue or invoke.

2)   Establish and document rules and procedures for the organization and operation of the Board, including any subgroups, and for the format and content of oral and written reports to and by the Board.

3)   Designate any representatives, consultants, experts, liaison officers, or other individuals who may be required to support the activities of the Board and define the duties and responsibi-lities of those persons.

6.   **MEMBERSHIP**

The chairperson, other members of the Board, and supporting staff are designated in the Attachment.

7.   **MEETINGS**

The chairperson will arrange for meetings and for such records or minutes of meetings as considered necessary.

8.   **ADMINISTRATIVE AND OTHER SUPPORT**

a. JPL will provide for office space and other facilities and services that may be requested by the chairperson or designee.

b. All elements of NASA will cooperate fully with the Board and provide any records, data, and other administrative or technical support and services that may be requested.

9.   **DURATION**

The NASA OSS AA, as the appointing official, will dismiss the Board when it has fulfilled its responsibilities.

10.   **CANCELLATION**

This appointment letter is automatically cancelled 1 year from its date of issuance, unless otherwise specifically extended by the approving official.

Edward J. Weiler

Enclosure

Distribution:
S/Dr. E. Huckins
S/Dr. C. Pilcher
SD/Mr. K. Ledbetter
SD/Ms. L. LaPiana
SD/Mr. S. Brody
SR/Mr. J. Boyce
SPR/Mr. R. Maizel
SPR/Mr. J. Lee
Q/Mr. F. Gregory
QS/Mr. J. Lloyd
JPL/180-904/Dr. E. Stone
JPL/180-704/Dr. C. Elachi
JPL/180-703/Mr. T. Gavin
JPL/230-235/Mr. R. Cook
JPL/264-426/Mr. C. Jones
JPL/180-904/Mr. L. Dumas
MCO FIB Board Members, Advisors, Observers, and Consultants.

Mars Climate Orbiter (MCO) Failure Investigation Board (FIB)

Members

MSFC/Mr. Arthur G. Stephenson Chairperson
> Director,
> George C. Marshall Space
> Flight Center

HQ/Ms. Lia S. LaPiana   Executive Secretary
> SIRTF Program Executive
> Code SD

HQ/Dr. Daniel R. Mulville   Chief Engineer
> Code AE

HQ/Dr. Peter J. Rutledge   Director,
(ex-officio)   Enterprise Safety and Mission Assurance
   Division
> Code QE

GSFC/Mr. Frank H. Bauer   Chief
   Guidance, Navigation, and Control Center
   Code 570

GSFC/Mr. David Folta   System Engineer
   Guidance, Navigation, and Control Center
   Code 570

MSFC/Mr. Greg A. Dukeman   Guidance and Navigation Specialist
   Vehicle Flight Mechanics Group
   Code TD-54

MSFC/Mr. Robert Sackheim   Assistant Director for Space Propulsions
   Systems
   Code DA-01

ARC/Dr. Peter Norvig   Chief
   Computational Sciences Division

Advisors: (non-voting participants)

Legal Counsel: Mr. Louis Durnya
   George C. Marshall Space Flight Center
   Code LS01

Office of Public Affairs: Mr. Douglas Isbell
   NASA Headquarters
   Code P

Consultants:

Ms. Ann Merwarth NASA/GSFC-retired
   Expert in ground operations and flight
   software development

Dr. Moshe F. Rubinstein, Prof. Emeritus,
                    UCLA, Civil and Environmental
                    Engineering

Mr. John Mari   Vice-President of Product Assurance
                           Lockheed Martin Aeronautics

Mr. Peter Sharer   Senior Professional Staff
                                Mission Concepts and Analysis Group
                                The Johns Hopkins University
                                Applied Physics Laboratory

Mr. Craig Staresinich   Program management and Operations Expert
                                TRW

Dr. Michael G. Hauser   Deputy Director
                                Space Telescope Science Institute

Mr. Tim Crumbley   Deputy Group Lead
                               Flight Software Group
                               Avionics Department
                               George C. Marshall Space Flight Center

Mr. Don Pearson   Assistant for Advanced Mission Design
                                Flight Design and Dynamics Division
                                Mission Operations
                                Directorate
                                Johnson Space Center

JPL/Mr. John Casani   (retired) Chair of the JPL MCO special review board

*JPL/Mr. Frank Jordan   Chair of the JPL MCO independent peer
                               review team*

*JPL/Mr. John McNamee   Chair of Risk Assessment Review for MPL
                               Project Manager for MCO and MPL
                               (development through launch)*

*HQ/SD/Mr. Steven Brody   MCO Program Executive
(ex-officio)   NASA Headquarters*

*MSFC/DA01/Mr. Drew Smith   Special Assistant to Center Director
                                   George C. Marshall Space Flight
                                   Center*

*HQ/SR/Dr. Charles Holmes   Program Executive for Science
                                   Operations
                                   NASA Headquarters*

*HQ/QE/Mr. Michael Card   Program Manager
(ex-officio)   NASA Headquarters*

Acronym list

AA = Associate Administrator
AACS = Articulation and Attitude Control System
AMD = Angular Momentum Desaturation
EDL = Entry, Descent, Landing
GDS = Ground Data System
ICD = Interface Control Document
ISA = Incident, Surprise, Anomaly
JPL = Jet Propulsion Laboratory
lbf-s = pounds (force)-second
LESF = Lander Entry State File
LIDAR = Light Detection and Ranging
LMA = Lockheed Martin Astronautics
MCO = Mars Climate Orbiter
MGS = Mars Global Surveyor
MIB = Mishap Investigation Board
MOI = Mars Orbital Insertion
MOS = Mission Operations System
MPL = Mars Polar Lander
MSOP = Mars Surveyor Operations Project
MSP = Mars Surveyor Program
MSP'98 = Mars Surveyor Project '98
NASA = National Aeronautics and Space Administration
NPD = NASA Policy Directive
NPG = NASA Procedures and Guidelines
N-s = Newton-seconds
NST = Near Simultaneous Tracking
OSS = Office of Space Science
PDT = Pacific Daylight Time
SCAM = Star Camera Attitude Maneuver
SIS = System Interface Specifications
TCM = Trajectory Correction Maneuver
UTC = Universal Time Coordinated
V&V = Verification and Validation
ΔV = Velocity Change